Scotty

WHY SCOTTY?

II Cor 4:8-10

Why Scotty? by Wynell Hunt and Terry Hill, © 1992 by Full Court
Press, P.O. Box 141513, Grand Rapids, Michigan 49514. All rights
reserved. No part of this publication may be reproduced, stored in a
retrieval system, or transmitted in any form or by any means– electronic,
mechanical, photocopy, recording or otherwise– without the permission
of the publisher.

1 2 3 4 5 6 Printing/Year 97 96 95 94 93 92

Printed in the United States of America

ISBN 0-9634057-3-X

WHY SCOTTY?

by *Wynell Hunt*
with Terry Hill

Table of Contents

Dedication

THIS BOOK IS DEDICATED to my family, Jimmy, Donna, Bobby and Scotty. Also I would like to thank those special family members and friends who listened to us as we voiced our fears and frustrations and still supported us in countless ways.

Acknowledgements

IT'S IMPOSSIBLE to list everyone who has supported during Scotty's ordeal. The following is a short list of those we do wish to acknowledge:

Bryan College's student body, faculty and staff for their faithful prayers and support.

Betty Wilkes and the ICU nurses at Jackson Hospital in Montgomery, Alabama.

Martha Turner, Mandy Merkel, Dr. Feinberg, Dr. Belsky and the great nurses and therapists at North Fulton Rehab Center.

Shannon Mize, M.D., family doctor and friend.

Dr. Steven Wolf, Physical Therapist at Emory University who worked so faithfully to encourage Scotty.

Diane Wahler and the people in Special Education at the University of Georgia.

Kent Robson, FCS (Family Consultation Service) Urban Ministries in Atlanta, and the friends who have faithfully supported Scotty's ministry with FCS.

CHAPTER ONE
What A Junior Year!

SCOTTY HAD just finished his Junior year at Bryan College, and what a year it was! He had been captain of the basketball team while attending Clarkston High School which is located in a suburb of Atlanta and had always played baseball since he was a small child. When he got to Bryan, he played intramural basketball, but never did try out for the college basketball team.

One of his professors, Rick Hughes, knew Scotty was a good athlete and talked him into trying out for the baseball team. And try out he did! Scotty became a premier second baseman and was chosen All-Conference his Sophomore and his Junior year. He was even honored as the outstanding pitcher on his team.

While keeping a very active daily athletic schedule, Scotty managed to make the Dean's List as a business administration major each of his past three years in college. He had a beautiful Christian girlfriend, and most important of all to his parents, Scotty had a real desire to serve God. What more could any Christian parents ask for?

Scotty came home at the end of the school year in May, and was considering his job opportunities for the summer while catching up on his water skiing skills at our home on Lake Lanier in Cumming, Georgia. The phone rang one evening, and one of Scotty's favorite professors from Bryan, Rick Hill, was calling him.

"Scotty, I'm spending the summer working with kids at Camp Victory over in Alabama," Professor Hill explained. "We are in desperate need of another senior counselor and I immediately thought of you. Do you think you might be interested in working here for the summer?"

Scotty didn't even hesitate. "Yes sir, when do I start?" he shot back.

"Well, it's about a four hour drive from Atlanta. How soon can you get here?" Rick asked.

"I'll be there tomorrow," Scotty answered. "This is great! See you tomorrow."

"Wait a minute, Scotty. Maybe I should give you directions to the camp," Professor Hill replied before Scotty hung up the phone.

When Scotty Hunt knew what to do, he didn't take much time in doing it. The next day he was off to Samson, Alabama, to begin the most eventful summer, yet, of his young life.

Camp Victory was a beautiful Christian camp sponsored by the Children's Bible Mission. It was situated in the beautiful green pine thickets of southern Alabama. Each year the Children's Bible Mission rewarded boys and girls for attending Bible clubs and memorizing Scriptures during the school year. Scotty's deep love for the Lord and kids helped him to become one of the camper's favorite counselors from the first day he arrived.

Scotty loved every day at Camp Victory and especially what the Lord had been teaching him there. He called home one evening in late July and told us that he really felt the Lord was calling him into some type of full-time Christian work with youth. He had always had a special place in his heart for kids, but now he knew God wanted him to work with them for his life's vocation. Jimmy, Scotty's father, and I were elated our child had been called into full-time Christian service. Words can't express how happy and proud we were of Scotty's decision.

One of Scotty's assignments as a camp counselor was to drive from the camp into the city of Samson for supplies or whatever was needed. On August 1, 1985, Scotty and two other counselors, Jeff Nelson and John Jackson, were to travel into town to pick up some watermelons for an afternoon picnic at the camp.

Jeff volunteered to drive his car and Scotty climbed into the back seat of the two-door late model Buick Regal. John was about to get into the front seat when he remembered he had forgotten his wallet. Scotty realized his six foot body could fit more easily into the front passenger's seat than John's six foot five inch frame. So, Scotty moved into the front seat to allow John more room to stretch out his long legs in the back seat. When John returned, he thanked Scotty and they were on their way into town.

Scotty always buckled his seat belt. It was a routine that he had practiced long before he had received his driver's license. But this particular day he did not.

The three friends joked and talked about daily activities at the camp as they drove into Samson at about nine thirty that morning. Then the unthinkable happened.

Jeff looked up from behind the steering wheel to notice a dog walking right down the middle of the road. He swerved his car to the right to avoid hitting the dog and his right front wheel slid off the pavement. He jerked the steering wheel back to his left and the car immediately streaked across the highway.

Then to all of the boys' complete horror, they saw another vehicle heading straight for the passenger side of their car. There was nothing they could do to avoid the collision except to brace themselves.

Scotty's quick reflexes told him to draw his knees up into his chest and hold on to whatever he could. Those were Scotty's last thoughts as the fast traveling automobile smashed head-on into the passenger side of Jeff's car.

About thirty minutes later, Jim Miller, the Camp Victory Director, received a call informing him of a bad accident involving three of his counselors. Without delay Jim jumped into his car and sped off to the accident scene. Rick Hill, Scotty's college professor, heard about the accident a few minutes later and quickly drove the short distance from the camp to the wreck.

When Rick arrived at the location, he saw Jeff and John standing near the demolished car. They had received minor injuries. Scotty was not as fortunate. He was still in the car, unconscious, as the paramedics and rescue personnel worked feverishly to open the door and free him.

About an hour after the accident, the door was finally pried open and Scotty was whisked off in an ambulance to the local county hospital. Rick Hill was in close pursuit and followed them all the way there.

The doctors at the hospital examined Scotty and immediately surmised that he had massive head injuries. There was nothing they could do, so they sent him on to Montgomery's Jackson Hospital.

Rick Hill tried desperately to reach us by phone time after time during the day, but we were sightseeing in Helen, Georgia, with Jimmy's cousin. We arrived home at four thirty and the phone was ringing when we walked into the house. Jimmy's face turned white as he listened to the news of his son's accident. He had sustained a brain injury, was in a coma, and his right side was paralyzed.

We dropped everything on the living room floor and I immediately ran to my neighbor's house, two doors away. Eleanor MacDonald had been a second mom to Scotty for several years and is a great woman of prayer. Her son, Aaron, had been a close friend of Scotty's since they were very young. I just had to get some friends praying for Scotty. As I ran to their house, I kept praying, "God, please don't let him be paralyzed."

When I rushed into their backyard, I could see the whole MacDonald clan gathered on the lakeshore having a family reunion. I explained the news about Scotty and they immediately gathered around me and lifted me up in prayer. It was so reassuring to have friends like these.

All the way to Montgomery, I continued to pray, "Lord, just don't let him be paralyzed. Please don't let him be paralyzed."

We arrived in Montgomery at about eight thirty and were greeted by Rick who introduced us to Dr. Hackman. Dr. Hackman informed us it was a frontal lobe injury that would probably leave him paralyzed for life on his right side. Except for a slight cut on his chin that required three stitches, Scotty looked perfectly normal.

As we exited Scotty's room, I was crying profusely when a complete stranger approached me. Her name was Ruth Johnson and she said she had seen them bring Scotty into the emergency room. She was a Godly woman of about sixty years of age who then reached out her arms and hugged me close. She told me that this was a good hospital and that we had a good doctor. She was truly an angel of mercy. I am so thankful God sent her to minister to me that night. I turned and saw my husband, Jimmy, leaning his head up against the wall. Tears were streaming down his face.

Jimmy is a Delta Air Lines Captain and former Air Force pilot — always in control, always ready to give commands to remedy any situation. I went over and we just hugged each other as we cried together.

For the first time I could see the look of sheer helplessness on Jimmy's face. His mind cried out to God, "Why Scotty? Why not me? Why not anyone else, but Scotty? He loves You more than any kid I know. Why Scotty?"

CHAPTER TWO

The Jimmy Hunt Family

I HAD GROWN UP in a Christian home in Bristol, Florida. Jimmy grew up in Monroe, Louisiana, where he and his family were members of the First Baptist Church. He lived there until he joined the Air Force in his late teens. He was a very good airman and was invited to take the test to go to flight school and become an officer and pilot He was sent to Graham Air Force Base near Marianna where we met on a blind date. A short time later we were married and literally spent the next seven years living all over the world.

Along the way God blessed us with our first child, Donna, who was born in Quincy, Florida. Then our son, Bobby, was born while we were stationed at Travis Air Force Base in

California. Scotty came along while we were stationed in North Carolina, six years after his sister and four years after his brother.

Jimmy's career was exciting and sometimes very dangerous. He was involved in one mission where he dropped Belgian Paratroopers from his C-130 aircraft to rescue missionaries who were being held hostage in the Congo. These missionaries barely escaped execution. A few had already died before the paratrooper drop.

It was about at this interval in our lives that Jimmy decided it was time to get out of the military and start spending his life with his family. He applied for a position with Delta Airlines and was selected to attend their pilot training school. We were ecstatic and couldn't wait to make the move to Atlanta.

We made the move to Atlanta when Scotty was a year old. From his earliest years Scotty loved to throw a ball. This was the beginning of a great love for athletics. He lived to play ball — any kind of ball.

While his older brother, Bobby, loved sports too, he was more serious about his studies in school. Bobby is now a successful oral surgeon in Atlanta. Bobby and Scotty were very close and enjoyed fierce competition in many backyard games. Our neighbor, Herb Edwards, owned a vacant lot between our houses. Many ballgames and fights took place on that special piece of property.

Donna, our oldest, was a typical teenager, but one who had a sincere desire for spiritual matters. She even attended seminary where she met her husband who is now a minister. Donna was also Scotty's second mother and always advised him whether he wanted advice or not.

Scotty played every kind of ball he could get his hands on. He played baseball, football and basketball from the first day he was old enough to join the team. I can't even begin to count the number of times I took Scotty to practices and games.

When he got into junior high school, Scotty decided he was going to drop all sports except for basketball. He attended several basketball camps and clinics and was dead set on being an NBA All-Star after a very successful college career. His NBA hopes disappeared when he was a high school senior at barely five feet nine inches tall and a ringing wet one hundred and thirty-five pounds. But he still loved basketball and gave it one hundred and ten percent.

His senior year he was the captain of the Clarkston High School Angoras for twenty-three of the twenty-five games. This honor was given to a player based on his previous game performance. Playing as the point guard, Scotty and one other player were the only white members of the team. That didn't bother Scotty, he loved people regardless of their color or background. He was even selected to the National Honor Society for keeping up his grades while he played basketball.

After high school graduation, Scotty was offered a scholarship to attend Dekalb Junior College in Decatur, a suburb of Atlanta. He wanted to attend college away from home, but probably would have gone to Dekalb until he got a call from an uncle about a small Christian college in the mountains of east Tennessee.

William Jennings Bryan College is a Christian liberal arts college located in Dayton, Tennessee. You might recall that Dayton was the location of the famous Scopes Trial in 1925. Bryan College was named in honor of William Jennings Bryan, the former U.S. Secretary of State and popular defender of the Christian faith.

Each year Bryan College has what is called a "caravan" at which prospective college students can stay on campus for three days to experience firsthand what college life is all about. Scotty really wasn't interested in this obscure little college, but thought the caravan might give him a little better perspective on what Christian colleges were like.

From the moment Scotty drove on to the gorgeous mountaintop campus, he fell in love with Bryan College. Not only was the picturesque campus incredible, the students at this place were the most loving, caring people he had ever met. He knew from the second day on, Bryan was the place for him to attend college.

The first day of college that fall, Scotty met three friends that remain close to this day. Jay Efird, Doug Sloan, Lewis Alderman and Scotty were almost inseparable during their college days at Bryan. That is until they all found girlfriends. But even then, when they weren't with their girls, their girls knew where they could be found. Scotty brought them to our home in Georgia on many occasions for water skiing and "Mom's" home cooking. What a great bunch of guys — and girls!

Scotty still loved basketball, but decided not to play on the college team. He opted instead to play on an intramural squad with his buddies. Many students said that Bryan's intramural team could go toe to toe with the college varsity team. The varsity traveling team wisely never gave them the chance to find out.

During Scotty's sophomore year, Bryan's baseball team was short a few players and Coach Rick Hughes coaxed Scotty into playing. Coach Hughes says he was very pleasantly surprised at how adept Scotty was at baseball. At the end of his sophomore season, Scotty won the most improved player. Considering he came from a non-player to one of the best players on the team, this was a pretty good accomplishment.

Scotty's junior year brought more promise and hope for a very bright future when he made the Dean's List for the sixth consecutive semester with his major in business administration. In baseball Scotty played second base again and was selected All-Conference. He even developed into quite a nifty pitcher, too, and won the Pitcher of the Year award for Bryan.

Scotty also grew spiritually during his years at Bryan. Through the chapel services, the influence of Christian friends and his own quiet time, Scotty wanted nothing more than to serve God with all his heart.

And now the chance to share his life with kids at a Christian camp. Life just couldn't get any better than this for Scotty Hunt.

CHAPTER THREE

Thank God for Friends and Prayer

AS JIMMY AND I STOOD there in the Montgomery hospital hugging each other so very tight, we felt a complete pouring out of God's Spirit come upon us. We knew all at once that God was in control, even when we couldn't be. He would take control of this adversity, if we would only let Him. However, we had no idea of all the small hills and huge valleys He would lead us through.

We will always be grateful to my sister, Wynette Peacock, and her husband, John, who arrived at the hospital just an hour after we did. John, who had been like a brother to Jimmy, was a great comfort to him. My only sister, Wynette, and I are so very close. By just being with us, they will never know how much they helped.

Our two families had enjoyed vacations together for many years at the beach in Panama City. In fact just the week before the accident, Scotty had spent the weekend with them. Scotty always felt the Peacocks' house was his second home.

Then on the weekend, Jimmy's parents and his brother and sister drove all the way from Louisiana to be with us. Words can't express how much family and friends mean in a time like that.

The next day our daughter, Donna, arrived from Atlanta. Our son, Bobby, and his wife drove all the way from Augusta where he was in residency at the Georgia Medical School. Having the whole family together was a great comfort.

Scotty made some movements which gave us some hope that his injury was not as severe as the doctor had thought. Then the next day, we watched Scotty move all four limbs and even scratch his nose. This was very encouraging. Even his doctor called these movements very good signs.

Family and friends came from all over the South to visit and encourage us, and they did. I really don't want to think about what we would have done without the support of these loving, caring family members and friends.

About four days after the injury, Scotty began to show signs of posturing. This happens when the body becomes rigid and inflexible. Dr. Hackman then confirmed our greatest fears — Scotty probably had a brain stem injury. The injury could not be seen on the catscan, but Dr. Hackman made the diagnosis anyway based on Scotty's posturing.

On Monday I was left alone in Scotty's room for everyone had to return home. Jimmy had to be in Atlanta for the day. Then two very close friends, Julie Cullen and Linda Springer, drove for four hours to spend the day with me. During that entire week, we were amazed at how many friends and former neighbors traveled to be with us. Many pastors and churches in the Montgomery area heard of our plight and came to minister to us, also. God was so good!

The nurses inserted feeding tubes into Scotty's nose and I saw raw blood discharged. Then Scotty began to run a high fever which the doctor related to a broken thermostat inside his body. A cold thermal blanket was placed over him to try to bring his fever down.

We wanted to move him to Northside Hospital in Atlanta, but Dr. Hackman refused to give us permission as long as Scotty was in this condition. If we could only get him back to Atlanta, we believed everything would be better. We could only visit Scotty for ten minutes every hour and ten days after his accident I was very discouraged. On this particular night as I was leaving his room, a male nurse named Pat approached me.

He said, "Mrs Hunt, you need to look up what the word faith means."

I went back to my room and began reading Hebrews, chapter 11 in my Bible.

> "Now faith is the substance of things hoped for, the evidence of things not seen." (NKJV)

That verse greatly encouraged me. I also read Psalm 91:14-16 and they stood out as though they were meant for Scotty alone. I even wrote Scotty's name in certain places.

> "Because Scotty has loved me, therefore I will deliver him. I will set Scotty securely on high because he has known my name. Scotty will call upon me and I will answer him. I will be with Scotty in trouble. I will rescue and honor Scotty. With a long life I will satisfy Scotty and let Scotty behold my salvation." (KJV)

I can't begin to tell you how much these and other Scriptures from God's Word encouraged me.

A friend asked me why the accident could not have happened to him instead of Scotty. This friend had had accidents while under the influence of alcohol. He also knew the respect Scotty had for his relationship with God. I was able to share the plan of salvation with this friend, who might not have ever listened, otherwise.

Finally on Tuesday morning, August 13th, Dr. Hackman gave us permission to move Scotty to Atlanta. Jimmy and I were so excited to be taking Scotty back home. The next morning the ambulance arrived and we were ready to begin the transfer. I had noticed that Scotty was very pale, but had no idea that this might cause any complications.

We were then told that he was hemorrhaging from a stress ulcer in his stomach and he would have to be given five pints of blood. We were immediately frightened because of all the media attention given to the spread of AIDS through blood transfusions. Rock Hudson's episode with AIDS was taking place at this time.

Jimmy had the same blood type as Scotty and asked if he could donate his blood. The doctor replied that there was not enough time for him to do so. He assured us that this blood had been tested for AIDS and was very safe. We had no choice, but to trust God.

Scotty was given the blood and by evening, he began getting his color back. A gastroentrologist confirmed that he did indeed have an active bleeding ulcer. It could, however, be controlled by increasing his Tagament dosage.

Again, we showed up with the ambulance the next day to move Scotty to Atlanta. As we wheeled him out on the cart, we explained to him what we were doing just as though he were conscious. We had been told he couldn't hear us. We had persisted in talking to him from the first day of the accident, reading the Bible and playing Christian music that he loved, while we were in his room.

There was a nurse we nicknamed Sarge, because of her unwavering protectiveness of all of the ICU patients. As we rolled Scotty out of ICU, she had tears in her eyes as she told him good-bye.

Then a lady appeared to us out of the clear blue and asked if the young man on the stretcher was mine. After telling her yes, she pressed a book into my hand and said, "I was bringing this book to another patient, but you need it more. My name and address is inside the front cover and you can return it to me when you're finished."

I thanked her for the book, even though I didn't have any idea what it was about. It turned out to be the story of another person who had recovered from a coma. This book proved to be a real encouragement to us.

We loaded Scotty into the ambulance and his girlfriend rode inside while Jimmy and I followed close behind in our car. The ambulance traveled at more than eighty-five miles an hour, so the trip to Atlanta didn't take too long.

After arriving at Northside Hospital and having Scotty admitted into their Immediate Care facility, we waited for the doctor to come and give us some encouraging news. While in the waiting room, we met Larry and Judy Burkett. Larry is a Christian author and commentator on finances. Their son, Danny, had also been in an automobile accident and was here in Northside Immediate Care.

Danny had serious internal injuries and his life was still in jeopardy day by day. Even in the midst of their troubles, the Burketts made time to encourage us. Their hope, as was ours, was in the Lord.

I sincerely believed if we could just get back home and sleep and eat in our own house, everything would be O.K. What a disappointment! I almost fell apart in my bed that first night at home, when the stark realization hit me — nothing had changed. Now, I really had to accept the fact that there was nothing I could do to change what had already happened. There was no one on earth who could change the situation.

The next morning, Jimmy and I talked to the neurosurgeon, Dr. Bill Moore. After completing another catscan, he confirmed Dr. Hackman's diagnosis of a brain stem injury. Somehow, we had hoped the new doctor would give us different news. Not only did he give us bad news, he had nothing but negative comments with absolutely no encouragement.

Later that day, our family doctor, Shannon Mize, came to see us and told us not to hesitate to call and ask him any questions about medical procedures we didn't understand. And call Dr. Mize we did! Many times throughout this whole ordeal.

Then on Saturday, August 17th, the day nurse gave us some encouraging news. She believed she had seen Scotty's eyes open. That sure was great news.

Oh how thankful and blessed we were to have such great Christian friends visit us. Fellow members from our current church, First Baptist of Cumming, as well as old friends from our former church, First Baptist of Atlanta, as well as friends from our old neighborhood in Stone Mountain gave us tremendous support. They gave us such a fantastic outpouring of support. Now, it really was good to be back home.

On Sunday I was really convinced that Scotty was responding to my voice through twitches in his muscles. Dr. Moore told me it was all in my head — Scotty was still in a deep coma.

Scotty's vital signs stabilized and he was moved from intensive care to the neurological unit. Our new day nurse, Barbara, was so kind and positive about Scotty's condition. It was so good to see someone in the medical field that was an encouragement.

Jimmy started back to work at Delta training pilots. This helped some in keeping his mind on other things besides Scotty.

A few days later, the nurse began to put Scotty in a wheel chair, even though he was still very much in a coma. I still believed Scotty could hear us talking to him, so we continued to read Scripture and play his favorite Christian music. We even read the sport's pages to him.

About three weeks after his accident, Scotty began flailing around and appeared very active. That night before Jimmy and I left for home, we both talked to Scotty by leaning very close to his ear. As we did this, we believed we had heard a moaning sound from Scotty. When we told the doctor, he again assured us we were just hearing things. When a person is in a deep coma, you don't know whether they will ever hear, see or talk again. We were searching for any sign that would let us know Scotty was inside there.

The next day we had a substitute nurse who was very discouraging. Dr. Moore had informed us we should be looking for a nursing home to care for Scotty, because he would never be able to take care of himself. This nurse agreed completely with the doctor. This, we did not want to hear.

On Monday morning, August 26th, both of Scotty's eyes were wide open. He kept them open off and on for more than thirty minutes. I really believed something good was about to happen. Jay Cullen, a close friend, and Jimmy took Scotty on a wheelchair ride for the first time outside of his room.

Saturday, August 31st, was Scotty's twenty-first birthday. You will not believe the party his classmates from Bryan gave him. They brought gifts and posters from other classmates and even ate ice cream and cake in his room. His leg moved constantly throughout their visit as if he was really trying to respond to them.

Daily, from the day we first arrived, Scotty had received physical therapy. Today, the therapist said Scotty was very relaxed. Dr. Moore came to visit and reassured us that he didn't think Scotty would ever come out of his coma. He repeated his assertion that we find a good nursing home. We were discouraged, again.

That evening the deacons from our church came and had a special prayer for Scotty. Then some friends from Rehoboth Baptist Church, who had a son who had been in a coma and revived, came to visit. What an encouragement! God is so good!

CHAPTER FOUR
Miracles Never Cease

ABOUT FOUR WEEKS after the accident, Jimmy and I were a little frustrated that Scotty was not responding like we felt he should be. We called some of his friends at Bryan College and they organized an all night prayer vigil for Scotty's improvement. The next morning we went into the room and could not believe our eyes. For the first time Scotty seemed to be responding to our commands. We called the kids from Bryan and thanked them profusely while at the same time praising God. The doctors from Northside still ignored it.

Almost every day, we saw signs Scotty was responding to more commands from us. These were so enlivening to us, and again, we thanked God for the improvement.

We had heard of North Fulton Rehab Center and the tremendous successes they were having with patients like Scotty. Jimmy and I visited there and for the first time in my life I related to all those people in wheelchairs and beds. Before that day I probably would have run away in disgust at the sight I saw there. Now, I was so inspired at their sight to know that they had all at one time or another been in a coma. They weren't running around, but they were moving.

Dr. Feinberg, of the North Fulton Rehab Center, stopped by to check on Scotty. He told us that Scotty still was not out of his coma enough to begin rehab at his center, but that he would stop by in about a week to examine him again.

It's truly amazing how much little things mean. For example, the nurse removed his catheter and put pampers on him. Scotty was able for the first time to urinate on his own. We were so excited and happy.

On another day, Jimmy placed his hand in front of Scotty's eyes and Scotty blinked. Jimmy repeated this on twenty different occasions that day and each time, Scotty blinked his eyes. We were convinced he was getting better.

Jimmy made calls all over the country to find out how other brain injured patients had responded to different unorthodox treatments. He was determined to pursue every possible avenue to learn any knowledge that might help his son. We even came up with a few ideas of our own.

When patients are in a coma, their feet have a tendency to stretch forward and the toes to point, a position called "toe point." When the patient eventually does come out of a coma, he may have to have surgery to correct this. Jimmy thought maybe if we put high top tennis shoes on Scotty, this might help prevent that problem from occurring. So there was Scotty with high top Converse tennis shoes on the feet of that skinny little body. What a sight to behold!

Dr. Moore had incessantly told us that transferring Scotty to the North Fulton Rehab Center would be a waste of time. At first he wouldn't even allow Dr. Feinberg to examine Scotty. After much insistence on our part, he finally relented.

A few days later, Dr. Feinberg stopped by and told us he was convinced Scotty was definitely coming out of his coma. He would be ready for North Fulton Rehab Center very soon. We were so excited we couldn't contain ourselves.

Scotty began pulling his tube from his nose and had to be restrained. The restraining of his left hand really seemed to frustrate him. Finally, he pulled the tube out and the nurse just left it out. She tried feeding him ice cream and he ate just about the whole cup.

That same day he seemed to be very relaxed as he ran his fingers through his hair and even reached up and touched his Daddy's ear. Then Dr. Feinberg came by to examine Scotty once again. He gave us the most wonderful news we had heard since the accident. Scotty wasn't out of his coma, yet, but he was ready to begin rehab. Oh how we rejoiced!

A few days later, Scotty was transferred to North Fulton Rehab Center. We sat in the waiting room for a long time and began to get a little impatient when in bounced this sweet lady headed straight for us.

She said, "I'm the dietician here and I've come to see Scotty Hunt. We have been praying for him for several weeks."

Jimmy and I both were amazed and asked who she was.

"My name is Martha Turner and I will be working with Scotty to get him taking the kind of nourishment he needs. Our church has been praying for Scotty and I am so happy to finally meet him."

Then we met the speech therapist who would be working with him. Mandy Merkel was so sweet and informative about the daily procedures Scotty would be adhering to. She was a beautiful Jewish girl from South Africa with whom we immediately fell in love.

The first full day at the Rehab Center we say Scotty getting very frustrated from all the blood work and tests administered to him. Then Mandy, the speech therapist, asked Scotty to take a picture from her hand and hand it to me. Scotty did it — and not just once, but several times.

Every day he became a little more alert. He even nodded his head, yes, when asked if I was his mother. What a thrill that was to me!

A few days later, Dr. Feinberg asked for permission to place a feeding tube in his stomach. Scotty was still pulling the tube from his nose and having to have his hands restrained. Jimmy and I felt like having the stomach tube was a step backwards and were opposed to it. Dr. Feinberg thought it was too soon to feed him by mouth and somehow Scotty had to have his nourishment. The following morning we convinced Mandy to try feeding him. She agreed that she would begin the next day. That night Jimmy sneaked in some chocolate ice cream and fed it to Scotty. He ate all of it.

The doctor then agreed to forget the stomach tube if we could get Scotty to drink eight cans of high nutrient Ensure a day for nourishment. Jimmy and I vowed to make him do it and we did.

Now we had another problem. Scotty had begun biting people. It was probably due to his frustration of not being able to talk or communicate, but the doctor said he would have to have some type of head gear to keep him from hurting people.

One day as I was moving him over to his side he bit me. It hurt me more emotionally than physically. I prayed all the way home that night for God to allow this stage in his recovery to pass quickly.

On October 4th, Scotty whispered the word, Mom. He was also able to point to each member of his family in a picture. Dr. Feinberg asked him to say Mom, and he did it again.

He also began to tear his diaper off with his free hand. I had to literally potty train him all over.

Soon, Scotty was eating more and more solid food. He was consuming macaroni and cheese, hamburgers and french fries, and pancakes. He was coming out of his coma more and more.

His right hand was still postured and not moving at all. The doctor installed a balloon type mechanism on his arm to help straighten it. You could tell it was uncomfortable to Scotty and it probably caused him much pain. Rick Hill, Scotty's friend and professor at Bryan, called to see how he was doing. We told him about Scotty's right arm and Rick called another prayer meeting that night. The next morning Scotty was moving his right arm. Oh how we thanked God for Bryan

College, their students and all those who prayed so faithfully.

Just when you think things are really improving, something happens to break your spirit. Scotty bit another nurse pretty badly. And then shortly thereafter, Jimmy was taking him to the bathroom and Scotty bit his dad on the shoulder. Jimmy was so upset, he just sat Scotty down in his wheelchair and left the room.

What was really pitiful was the look on Scotty's face after he had bitten someone. You could see by his facial expressions he was so sorry and wanted to hug and kiss you. We sure hoped this would end soon.

To restrain his thrashing and uncontrollable moving, Scotty was placed in a posie which is similar to a straight jacket. Scotty hated it, but he had to wear it.

On October 2nd, Dr. Feinberg officially pronounced Scotty was out of his coma. It had been sixty-two days since the accident. Thank you, Lord!

CHAPTER FIVE
Out of the Coma

SCOTTY BEGAN EATING three full meals a day and waved his left hand good-bye to visitors. One friend even threw a wash cloth at him and Scotty threw it right back.

Then he began to speak audible words such as, "Hi, Mom" and "Hi, Dad." A couple of friends from Bryan visited him and he said, "Efird," in reference to his friend, Jay Efird.

On Sunday, October 27th, my daughter, Donna, and I took Scotty to Arby's for lunch. He had such a good time. We did as well. We went to visit some old friends and Scotty hugged them and actually cried real tears.

Then, Scotty began to get concerned about spiritual matters. He asked questions and wanted to pray many times with me, Jimmy and our pastor, Butch Franklin. Sometimes he was even afraid to go to sleep for fear he might not wake up.

Saturday, November 2nd, was a remarkable day in the Jimmy Hunt family. Scotty Hunt would be coming home for a day trip for the first time since the accident. His brother, Bobby, was there as well as the rest of his family. He knew his way around the house and thoroughly enjoyed his visit. When we finally took him back to the hospital, he was worn out. But he still wouldn't go to sleep, because he thought he would die.

We took Scotty to the opthomologist to have his eyes checked and found he had double vision and needed glasses. When we picked up the glasses, he was able to see much more clearly and was especially glad to watch ball games on television.

Scotty was to be the "best man" in Lewis and Terry Alderman's wedding. The wedding was to have taken place a week after the accident and Lewis wanted to postpone it, but we encouraged him to go on with it. When they visited Scotty at the Rehab Center, they brought a video tape of their wedding service. We watched a beautiful ceremony during which the pastor, Lewis' father, paid tribute to Scotty and even prayed for Scotty. We all cried together.

Scotty's premonition of death seemed to be waning and he was beginning to believe that he was going to get better. Even his prayers were more positive.

November 15th was my birthday. Scotty remembered it without being told and gave me the best present I could ever receive. As I walked into the room that morning he sang, "Happy Birthday" to me. What a present!

Scotty began walking with a walker and was improving more each day. He really wanted to walk and put every extra effort into it.

His favorite college football team was the Georgia Tech Yellow Jackets. He was looking forward to seeing them beat Georgia this year and thoroughly enjoyed the game on television. And yes, Tech did beat the Bulldogs.

The date of December 6th was set for his going home. He worked even harder in anticipation of his release from the Rehab Center. We went to eat at Perimeter Mall and Scotty was a little self-conscious of people staring at him, but he was glad to be going home for good.

Then on December 7th came the most significant day in Scotty's life since the accident. We drove Scotty to Bryan College where he had spent three great years forming friendships that are precious to him to this day.

As we approached the campus, we couldn't believe our eyes when we saw a huge twenty-foot banner welcoming Scotty. It brought tears to all of our eyes. Then, as we parked in front of the Administration Building, a crowed of more than a hundred Bryan students, faculty and staff had gathered to greet Scotty. What an incredible sight!

The students held a pizza party in Scotty's honor and Scotty ate pizza until he was almost sick. We watched the Bryan girls basketball team play in a tournament and then left for home at about eleven thirty that evening.

This short trip was rather bittersweet. Scotty loved seeing his friends who had been so faithful during his illness. And yet on the other hand, it brought back memories of how life used to be and never would be again.

CHAPTER SIX

North Fulton Rehab Outpatient

SCOTTY WAS BEING TREATED on an outpatient basis at North Fulton Rehab Center. He had physical therapy, occupational therapy and speech therapy each day. We would take him after breakfast and bring him home at about three thirty. This became our daily schedule for the next eight months.

We began to make videos of Scotty's progress. This was very encouraging for each time Scotty viewed the videos of his progress, he was more inspired to keep working harder to walk and talk like he used to. His real goal was to get well enough to go back to Bryan and finish his degree. He really loved Bryan College.

I remember watching Scotty strain every muscle in his body to get into the car one morning. Tears filled my eyes as I reminisced about the once strong legs and body he had had before. I needed to learn to put those thoughts out of my mind and remember how pitiful he was lying in the hospital in a coma compared to how far he had come. It's still tough to do that even today, but it can be done. I just have to believe in what God promises in Romans 8:28, "God causes all things to work for our good" (NASV) and will equip Scotty to do whatever He wants to accomplish in Scotty's life.

Scotty's right arm still needed extra therapy, so Dr. Belsky recommended a steel splint for Scotty to sleep in every night. The splint would cause his arm to be straight, even when Scotty was in a deep sleep.

Christmas Eve, 1985, was very meaningful in the Hunt household, for Scotty took ten steps by himself. Up to that point, he had always used a walker, but he was determined to walk without it as soon as possible.

A few days after Christmas, friends from Camp Victory came to visit Scotty at our house. For the first time we realized Scotty remembered every detail about the camp and even eating breakfast the morning of the accident. Getting into the car, however, was the last memory he could recall. Our daughter, Donna, left for Southwestern Baptist Seminary in Fort Worth, Texas, and though we encouraged her to leave, we missed her dearly. She was always such a help and encouragement to her dad and me as well as Scotty.

Our son, Bobby, has really had a harder time adjusting to Scotty's accident than any of us. He just couldn't accept how different Scotty is compared to the brother he used to play basketball and other sports with. Spiritually, he was struggling with why God would allow a guy like Scotty, who was doing His work, to go through something like this. What had happened to Scotty also seemed to be affecting his marriage adversely.

Scotty was still progressing. He started walking regularly with a walker on wheels he received from his therapist. He began eating full meals using his right hand. He even learned to tie a bow using both hands. Praise God!

We appreciated so much the excellent care he received from the doctors, nurses, therapists and other medical personnel. We know it would not have been possible, however, without God's great provision of grace.

On Friday, February 14th, we drove Scotty back up to Bryan College so he could take his girlfriend to their Valentine's Banquet. Scotty used his walker to escort his date to the dinner and had a great evening. Jimmy and I kept wondering how his girlfriend was accepting the "new Scotty." So far, she was doing very well.

The doctors told us Scotty's jaw was not aligned right and that we should see an oral surgeon. We naturally took him to his brother who was still in residency in oral surgery in Augusta. Bobby x-rayed Scotty and found that some of the nerves in his jaw had not healed and that was the reason for his slurred speech. He referred us to an oral surgeon in Atlanta for further tests.

Near the end of February, Scotty began walking using only a cane. Another small, but significant milestone had been achieved.

Jeff Nelson, the driver of the car in Scotty's accident, came for a visit. Scotty got to be alone with Jeff and explained time and again how Jeff shouldn't feel guilty for his condition. Scotty did his best to convince Jeff it was all in God's timing and will.

Scotty made great progress in walking with his cane. He would go up and down the halls of the therapy center visiting rooms and encouraging new patients who were in comas. He met a patient named Mark Malone who was in a stage in his coma where he was hitting people. Scotty talked to Mark's parents about his own biting stage and encouraged them that this would eventually pass. What a blessing to Jimmy and me to see Scotty encouraging others, just the way we were encouraged by others.

I started taking Scotty for walks along our street in Cumming. The neighbors all exclaimed how much it made their day to see him walking. He truly is a walking miracle!

We took a vacation to Florida in March and visited the Montgomery hospital where Scotty was first taken after his accident. We saw nurse Betty and she took Scotty's picture to show to her church family for they had been faithfully praying for him. Dr. Hackman even came out of surgery to greet us and marvel at Scotty's recovery.

The following Sunday, Scotty tied his own necktie without any assistance. Another small triumph to celebrate.

On April 11th, we took Scotty back to Bryan College for their Junior/Senior Banquet. You see, this was the class Scotty would have been graduating with. The banquet is a fancy dinner and an all-night party for the upper classmen where they dress in full tuxedos and deliver flowers to their dates. We left him there with his friends, Jay and Lewis, and his girlfriend. We were very apprehensive about leaving him, but were convinced it was time to do so. He had a great time.

Two of Scotty's therapists, Mandy and Sherry, accompanied us to Bryan to discuss Scotty's schedule for classes the following fall. Scotty was determined to return to Bryan and finish his degree. Mandy and Sherry were thoroughly impressed with Bryan's faculty and staff and agreed Scotty could attempt to return to college.

On April 16th, Scotty walked from the Rehab Center building all the way to the car without his cane. The trek seemed to take forever, but he finally did it and was so proud.

A few days later, Scotty was reaching for his cane and experienced a bad fall. He wasn't hurt physically, but emotionally his confidence was set back.

On May 4th, Terry and Lewis drove to Atlanta to pick Scotty up and take him back to Bryan to go on their Senior trip. Again, Jimmy and I were a little alarmed, but knew he had to go with them. When we met him later on in the week, we were greatly relieved to learn he had had a fantastic trip.

That evening we attended Vesper Services for the graduating seniors and their families. Of course, if not for the accident, this would have been Scotty's Vesper Service. Needless to say, he was very emotional and cried all the way through the service. During the service many slides were shown of the seniors, including Scotty. I'm sure this made it even tougher.

At the end of the service, the lights were turned off and each senior lit a candle. As they began to light their candles, a couple of

Scotty's friends walked to his seat, picked him up and carried him to the front of the Rudd Auditorium to light his own candle along with them. They even gave Scotty an honorary diploma. What a bittersweet moment this was for Scotty and for us, too!

The next day, Bryan's graduation ceremony was an incredible experience for Scotty. He cried and cried as he watched his fellow classmates receive their degrees. Then Dr. Karl Keefer, the Academic Dean of the college, had a special time of recognition for Scotty when he called out his name and had him stand. As he stood, the entire senior class of Bryan gave him a standing ovation. A friend commented that Scotty received more recognition than any of the members of the graduating class.

CHAPTER SEVEN

Reality
Sets in for Scotty

JIMMY HAD PROMISED the family a trip to Hawaii if and when Scotty ever came out of his coma. Two days after Bryan's graduation, Jimmy made good on his promise. Jimmy and I flew out on Sunday with Bobby and his wife. Scotty, his sister, Donna, her friend, Polly Cullen and Scotty's girlfriend met us in Honolulu on Tuesday. We greeted them with flowered leis and began a beautiful week in Hawaii.

Scotty tried to eat everything that was placed in front of him — Chinese, Japanese, American. It was just fantastic to see him eat so much.

A few days after we returned from Hawaii, Scotty's girlfriend called him. After he hung up the phone, we could tell he was really downhearted and we feared she was beginning to break off their relationship.

Jimmy had learned through his vast research of head injuries some very disheartening news which we hoped would not come true in Scotty's life. More than ninety percent of all spouses and romantic relationships with head injury patients end in separation.

Jimmy allowed him to drive our car down the street. Scotty remembered exactly how to manipulate each control in maneuvering the vehicle for his first stint behind the wheel.

It really distressed him to see friends do the things he used to do and no longer could — baseball, basketball. Then on Thursday, May 29th, when a couple of his friends were present, Scotty decided to try water skiing again. Before the accident he was an excellent water skier and especially proficient at slaloming.

I was so nervous when Scotty entered the water. I knew he could swim, but I was not so sure if he could water ski. One of his friends jumped into the water with him to help him adjust his skis. A few seconds later, his friend returned to the boat commenting Scotty didn't need help.

Jimmy started the engine very slowly and Scotty fell over to the side. After seven or eight tries, Scotty finally got up for only a few yards, but then fell again. He was very disappointed he couldn't go farther, but Jimmy and I were very pleased at his effort.

Scotty was very frustrated. His mind knew every detail of how to water ski, but his body just couldn't negotiate what his mind commanded.

By mid June, Scotty's persistence paid off. He could water ski for several hundred yards without falling. He really did enjoy it.

He worked very hard daily on improving his walking. We noticed his posture was improving and we could see his whole attitude changing for the better. His desire to walk normally outweighed his speech therapy practice.

Several patients and their parents came to our house on the lake for swimming and a picnic. Scotty's physical therapist, Peggy Webber, was thoroughly impressed with Scotty's water skiing prowess. Scotty even threw horseshoes with his right hand and had a fabulous day.

On Sunday, June 22nd, I took Scotty to the airport for him to fly to Little Rock, Arkansas, to visit his girlfriend. He walked down the jetway and onto the plane by himself. As I watched him sway from side to side with his cane, I couldn't help but cry tears of thankfulness at how far he had progressed. Thank you Lord!.

A few days later we met Scotty at the airport on his return trip from Little Rock. As soon as we saw him, we could see he was very discouraged. What we had feared had happened. His girlfriend just couldn't handle the new Scotty and had broken up with him.

After all he had been through, he was faced with yet another obstacle to overcome — loneliness and depression. After listening to some Christian tapes on dealing with depression and loneliness, Scotty seemed to bounce back from yet another setback. Thank you Lord!

Scotty and his dad have a very special relationship. They love each other like no other father and son, and yet they also can discourage each other. One afternoon Jimmy and Scotty went outside to pitch some ball and Scotty didn't especially want to. Scotty was still concerned over the loss of his girlfriend and Jimmy wanted to help him to get over it. When one of them is down, the other just can't handle it. They both wound up getting upset with each other and Jimmy eventually drove off in his truck to cool off. This was the first of many confrontations between Scotty and his dad. The good thing about the confrontations was that they always forgave each other and made up.

Scotty went with his dad and his cousin, John, to an Atlanta Braves game and walked to and from the stadium with no problems. He even got to see the Braves' Bob Horner hit four home runs in one game. The Braves still lost 11-8, however, but Scotty walked beautifully.

A few days later, another of Scotty's friends came over and Scotty drove the boat for his friend to ski. He pulled his buddy while he skied and even parked the boat at our dock which was quite an accomplishment — another sign that the real Scotty was returning.

Many times Scotty would get real down on himself. Some counselors from a local camp came over to enjoy the day at our house and on the lake. Scotty tried to make his way to the boat on a walkway extending about thirty feet over the surface of the water to the boat dock. The water was a little rough and he lost his balance and fell into the lake. He was more embarrassed than hurt. Later that evening, still feeling embarrassment from his fall, Scotty remarked that he wished God had just gone ahead and taken him to heaven from the accident. I wanted to say something to him, but there are times when even a mother needs to remain silent. This was one of them.

Rick Hill, Scotty's professor and friend from Bryan College, took him back down to the dock for a chat. After talking with Rick for a while, Scotty's attitude changed and he was back to his old fun-loving self again. Thank

God for Christian friends who loved and counseled Scotty.

Scotty began speaking and giving his testimony to several church youth groups. He has shared his story on some twenty to thirty different occasions. Jimmy and I have never heard him. He says it would make him nervous and as emotional as I am, I know I would always start crying and not be any help to him. Every time he speaks, I believe it pushes him a little more to work harder in his therapy.

In late July, we took a family vacation to Panama City, Florida. Scotty had so much fun and did so many exciting things. He and his cousin, John-John, caught a shark while fishing off the pier. He climbed aboard a large boat and spent a day deep-sea fishing with his dad and some of his family. They brought back more than ninety pounds of red snapper and grouper.

Then came a time of testing for me as they all wanted to go ride go-carts. Of course, Scotty wanted to drive, too, and I was very apprehensive. He watched the carts speed around several laps before spying the fastest one. When it was his turn to drive, he immediately jumped into the cart he thought was the fastest.

And it was the fastest by far. I almost cringed every time he would pass a friend and then turn around to see if they were gaining on him. I could just see him careening into the wall and someone blindsiding him. Such are a mother's thoughts after what we had been through. But I just had to let go and let Scotty be Scotty. He had a fantastic time and so did I once the ride was over.

Scotty ventured several times down to the pool by himself. This was a first, also. Jimmy and I watched from our window in the condo as Scotty walked up to complete strangers, struck up a conversation and continued the dialogue as they swam in the pool. More and more each day, the old Scotty kept coming back.

On Wednesday, August 6th, Scotty went to therapy and officially turned in his cane. It had been exactly one year and five days since the accident. He walked very slow, but without the cane that had been his constant companion for so many months.

Jimmy virtually turned our basement into a local gym for Scotty's rehabilitation. We had a treadmill, a punching bag and weights to help in his therapy. We tried different methods — some we had heard of from others and some we thought up ourselves — to help Scotty. We had him carry a glass of water around the house to let him see how level he was walking. Simple, yet day after day, Scotty saw his walking improve by that water moving less and less in that clear glass.

Another great form of therapy was video games. These helped Scotty to use both hands and thumbs as well as having fun playing games. It also enhanced his concentration for longer periods of time.

His water skiing has improved immensely. He is now skiing over the wake and is even slaloming — skiing with both feet on one ski. This has greatly increased his confidence and self-esteem.

Another of Scotty's major goals since coming out of the coma, was to return to Bryan College and finish his degree. We weren't quite sure if he was ready, but he was very determined to do so. If it were any other college, I would have been very opposed, but Bryan and its students had been so special to us and Scotty that we decided it was the right time and place.

The North Fulton Rehab Center gave Scotty a going away party. All of his former therapists and doctors attended. Several of them took pictures of Scotty as he walked through the front doors for the last time as a patient. As I looked back at their faces while walking to our car, I could see tears streaming down their cheeks.

On Sunday night, our church had a special service to send our college students back to school and seminary. Each of the six students gave a short testimony of their love and appreciation for the Lord and their home church. Scotty was last and spoke confidently and boldly of God's graciousness and goodness. Of course, I was very emotional, but as I scanned the congregation, I saw very few dry eyes. Our pastor gave an invitation to accept Jesus Christ as Lord and Savior or to rededicate lives for His service. More than thirty-five persons, most of whom were young people, responded to the Holy Spirit's bidding through Scotty.

Then, it was off to Bryan College for Scotty. Jimmy and I, as well as all his Atlanta friends, were going to miss him. We had tried to reteach him in one year what had taken eighteen years previously. He had become a child and grown into a man again, and now it was time to let go of him one more time.

The

Hunt

Family

Album

Family picture when Scotty was ten years old. (From left to right) Scotty, Bobby, Dad, Donna, Mom.

Scotty and two neighbor friends in the Clarkston Youth Football League. (From left to right) David Leathers, Scotty, Aaron MacDonald).

Scotty in his senior year at Clarkston High School as point guard.

Scotty in his senior year at Clarkston High School.

Scotty slaloming on Lake Lanier before his accident.

Spring break, Scotty's junior year at Bryan.

The highway on the way to Samson, Alabama where the accident took place.

August 1, 1985 - Nothing "Regal" about this wrecked Buick!

The passenger side of the car which had to be pried open to take Scotty out.

Scotty returned to Bryan December 7, 1985 for his first visit since the accident. Scotty was WELCOMED by students, faculty and staff.

Scotty's *real* graduation from Bryan, May 1990.

May 1990 - Scotty's *real* graduation from Bryan. (From left to right) Bill DeKlerk, Jay Efird, Scotty).

June, 1991 - (From left to right) Donna, his sister; Bobby, his brother, and Scotty.

CHAPTER EIGHT
Back to Bryan College

DRIVING ONTO THE BEAUTIFUL hilltop campus was needless to say, a bit melancholy. We loved this school beyond measure, and yet, we were going to have to entrust Scotty into their love and care while we lived more than one hundred fifty miles away.

We drove straight to his dorm and got all his clothes, stereo and other college stuff unpacked. I was a little alarmed his room was on the fourth floor in a dorm with no elevators, but this is where Scotty wanted to be. Like any well-meaning mother, I told him to remember to always use the handrail when walking up and down the stairs. Jimmy and Scotty both gave me the crazed-eye look as if to say, "Really, Mom."

His best friend, Jay Efird, would be the resident director in his dorm. We knew he would keep a close eye on Scotty and be there to help him whenever he needed him.

As we left the dining hall watching Scotty talking with friends, I wanted to go over and grab his hand and put him in the van to go back to Georgia with us. But I knew beyond a shadow of a doubt, this is where God wanted Scotty to be. It was also where Scotty really desired to be.

Jimmy and I walked to the van with tears in our eyes. But we also walked with the calm assurance that God would take good care of Scotty, even when we couldn't. As an old song says, "He didn't teach us to swim, just to let us drown."

After being at Bryan for a few days, reality set in for Scotty. It wasn't the same as it used to be, nor would it ever be again. He couldn't go to the gym and play basketball with his friends like he used to do. Most of his close friends had graduated and left him behind. His former girlfriend was still a student and he had to see her every day. He sincerely believed she would still be his girl, if he hadn't been in the accident. Mom and Dad would not be there to encourage him daily, like it was at home. Thank God for Jay Efird and Dr. Bill Brown, the Provost and Scotty's theology professor.

Labor Day weekend Scotty got a ride to Cartersville, Georgia, which is a short distance away from our home. Jimmy and I met him there and brought him home for his first visit since he left for Bryan more than three weeks before. His walking speed had picked up since he had to do so much walking back and forth to classes. It was great having him home.

Scotty was taking just one class this semester to see if he could do what he thought he could do. The class was Theology and his professor, Dr. Bill Brown, worked with him above and beyond the call of duty. Scotty took his first quiz and received a grade of seventy-five. He was very disappointed, because he thought he could earn the same grades he had previously before the accident.

I was really beginning to wonder if he had gone back to school too early. But I knew God would direct Scotty in doing what was right.

Donna, our daughter at seminary in Fort Worth, Texas, was getting married in December. Her fiancé, Dean Vonfeldt, a fellow classmate, called to ask us for her hand in marriage, and we gladly gave it. Dean was such a fine young man and still is an excellent son-in-law and father to our grandchildren. We called Scotty and he was very excited for his sister.

At mid-semester, we examined how far Scotty had come during the first weeks of school. He received high marks in our book for learning to adapt to new situations and environment. He had made higher grades before his accident, but he was progressing nicely.

Our son, Bobby, and his wife had a baby on November 18th, and named him Christopher Scott Hunt. The name Christopher came from a very close cousin of Bobby's and of course, Scott is from Scotty. Scotty was so excited to finally become an uncle.

Scotty took his final exam with much fear and trepidation before coming home for Christmas vacation. We were all elated to discover he had received a B+. Maybe he really could complete senior college work after all.

During Christmas vacation, Scotty rode a bicycle for the first time. He also drove Bobby's stick shift car and did very well. More and more milestones were being achieved every day.

When Scotty got back to Bryan to begin the second semester, he decided to take Theology and a marketing course which was required for his major. After two classes of the marketing course, he called home and told us it was about to kill him. A few days later, he dropped the marketing course.

Jimmy was upset. He wanted to bring Scotty home. But he got over it after talking to Dr. Belsky at the Rehab Center. Dr. Belsky told Jimmy that Scotty was able to do the work mentally, but emotionally just could not keep up with the requirements.

In January, 1987, I joined the Gwinnett Chapter of the National Head Injury Foundation. Dr. Feinberg of North Fulton Rehab Center was the speaker. I really felt that I needed to share my experiences of Scotty as well as hear other people's testimonies of how they coped.

Scotty had a couple of days off from school, so I drove to Bryan and picked him up and brought him home. One the return trip we listed to a cassette of an Evangelist named David Ring. Rev. Ring had had cerebral palsy from birth, but yet was speaking with his slurred speech across the nation and seeing people come to know Jesus Christ. Scotty and I both cried as we listened to this very moving tape. God really used that sermon by David Ring to bolster Scotty's confidence in the fact that God will use him if he will just keep himself available The best ability God is looking for is availability.

David Ring's speaking is no better than Scotty's and his walking is not as good. Yet, God has given David a wife, children and a ministry that blesses and encourages people all over this nation. Scotty was excited!

One day in March, Scotty called to inform us that he had tripped over his laundry basket the previous night and had to acquire nine stitches at the hospital. When the doctor told Scotty he needed nine stitches, Scotty retorted, "Why not just make it an even ten?" His sense of humor was definitely back.

When we heard of the accident, it really kind of shook Jimmy and me up. But Jay assured us he had been x-rayed and no further injuries had been received. We concluded he best keep his laundry basket in a different place.

The rest of the school year concluded without any major catastrophes. Scotty came home in early May to begin driver education classes with a lady named Ileana McCaique. What an incredible experience this would turn out to be!

We found a small Ford Tempo that was equipped with an air bag for Scotty to begin lessons. At first, Scotty was very discouraged because his right foot reflexes were not fast enough to begin training. Ileana was very tough and locked horns with Scotty on many occasions. Scotty didn't like her at all — until he passed the course and later was thankful for her thoroughness and persistence in doing things the right way with no shortcuts.

Scotty passed his driving tests enough to be allowed to drive during daylight hours with an adult in the front seat with him. Jimmy and I drove with him at every available opportunity to help him gain more experience behind the wheel of a car.

Scotty was really struggling with self-control of his emotions. Every day with his driving teacher meant another day of total frustration during and after the lesson. On one occasion, Scotty was driving us home and doing real well in heavy traffic, when he pulled the car over. He remarked that he was just too upset emotionally to continue driving home. He got into the back seat and then began to sob. He just could not understand why he couldn't better control his emotions.

Shortly thereafter, Scotty began seeing a Christian psychologist. The psychologist was better able to relate to Scotty's problems psychologically as well as spiritually than others he had seen. He also began talking regularly to our youth minister, Donald Wise. Donald gave him help and encouragement that Scotty will never forget.

Dr. John Bartlett, a professor at Bryan, was taking a group of students to Europe for a study tour. Scotty decided to go, thinking he could have a good time as well as get some needed college credits. We were very apprehensive about his traveling, especially overseas, but placed him in God's hands for protection.

He toured London, Paris, Holland, Lucerne, Switzerland, and parts of Italy. He called us one evening from Lucerene and related a story that scared me half to death.

It seems Scotty wasn't feeling well the previous day while in Paris, so he stayed in his hotel room while the rest of the group toured the famous art gallery, the Louvre. Later in the day, he began feeling better and decided to take a cab and tour the Louvre by himself.

After taking a self-guided whirlwind tour of the famous art gallery, he boarded a subway train for the trip back to his hotel. When he got off the train, he was completely lost and had no earthly idea which direction to walk toward his hotel.

Scotty stumbled around for a while trying to locate any landmarks that might be familiar. Every building and street were completely foreign to him. He didn't know the phone number, the address, nothing, except the name of the hotel. He said he even remarked to a bum lying on a bench, "I know you can't understand me, but save me a place because I'll probably be back in a little while to spend the night."

Then Scotty prayed and told the Lord he sure needed help in finding his way back to the hotel. He looked up and there stood a woman with a small child. Scotty approached her and to his utter delight found she spoke English. He asked her if she knew where his hotel might be and she exclaimed, "Why you're just two blocks away."

She then tried to explain to Scotty directions to get there. After listening for a few minutes, Scotty could not understand her. He very humbly asked her if she and her little boy could please walk with him to the hotel. Thank God for guardian angels, which we really believe that sweet lady was. He finally made it back to the hotel and thanked the lady profusely. What a trip!

In August of 1987, a short time before returning to Bryan for school, he passed the test that allowed him to drive at night. He was so excited to have this privilege again.

Scotty still wasn't using his right arm as much as he should. After talking with several persons bout this problem, one friend suggested he put his left arm in a sling. This would, of course, force Scotty to use his right arm. Scotty did this for several weeks and it greatly increased his right arm's mobility. This remedy sounded so simple, but yet it really worked. Thank you Lord!

On August 11th, Scotty and Jimmy drove to Ileana McCaique's for his final driving test. He passed and would now be able to drive by himself. I didn't mind his driving so much, as long as Jimmy or I were with him. But I had to let go a little bit more and give his driving safety completely over to God.

The time had come for Scotty to return to Bryan. I was really apprehensive about this school year for several reasons. His best friend and resident director in his dorm, Jay Efird, was married and gone. All of his other closer friends had graduated and married. This college year, Scotty would be more on his own than ever before.

Scotty insisted on taking four classes instead of the two we recommended. At the end of the first day, he called us and wanted to quit and come home. All he had left to gain his degree were business courses. And they were tough.

He was very frustrated with his assignments. What used to take him an hour to finish now required several hours of hard work. And when it was completed, he still didn't understand what he had done. More and more, I wondered if were going to be able to do it.

Then on November 2nd, Scotty's mindset hit rock bottom. He had completed a major take-home test and had given it to a friend to deliver to his professor's office. The test never got there. His friend said she was sorry and that she must have lost it. It was never found.

Scotty's professor suggested Scotty take the test over. As far as Scotty was concerned, it was a mute issue. That was the final straw. He called me and asked me to come take him home.

On the trip up to Bryan, I cried and prayed for wisdom and strength as I listened to

Christian praise tapes. The dream of finishing his degree was coming to a shattering halt.

It was a very tearful good-bye when Scotty and I drove off the Bryan College campus that cold day in November. What would be around the next turn in the life of Scotty Hunt? I certainly am thankful I had no earthly idea at that point.

CHAPTER NINE
More Therapy

A FEW DAYS LATER, Scotty visited Dr. Belsky at the Rehab Center to check into the possibility of more therapy. The center came up with a few new ideas and Scotty decided to try them.

We contacted Gainesville College which is just a few miles from our home in Cumming. We thought if Scotty could audit a course, it might boost his confidence in pursuing and finishing his degree. He decided to take an algebra class.

It was very interesting to discover an insight from one of Scotty's doctors, Dr. David Schwartz. He thought Scotty was concentrating too much on what he could not do, instead of concentrating more on what he could accomplish. Scotty really tried to put this advice into practice.

We attended the next meeting of the Head Injury Foundation in Gwinnett county. The speaker was Dr. Steven Wolf, a specialist in physical therapy for head injury patients at Emory University in Atlanta.

We later met with Dr. Wolf and were very impressed with his program. We asked if he could help Scotty and he agreed to do so. After meeting with Scotty, he told him he could expect more improvement for many years to come. He even remarked that running was within the realm of possibility for Scotty. That really got us all fired up to work even harder.

We discovered by visiting other Christian colleges, Scotty could get a degree in Christian Education with an additional thirty-four hours of credit. Scotty no longer had an interest in business, so he was considering changing his major. We visited Toccoa Falls College in Georgia and Southeastern Bible College in Birmingham. The people at each school were extremely nice, but I wasn't convinced either campus was the right place for Scotty.

Scotty finished his algebra course at Gainesville and received a ninety-seven. We were all very encouraged.

A few days later, Scotty was driving to therapy when a panel truck turned in front of him and hit his car. The driver of the truck jumped out and immediately began to apologize for hitting Scotty's car. He even told the police officer the accident was his fault and not Scotty's. The officer gave the truck driver a ticket and we thought that would be the end of the matter.

To quote a word popular among young people today — "Not!" When the truck driver's insurance company learned Scotty was a handicapped driver, they admitted no liability. Even in court the truck driver changed his story and made Scotty look as guilty as himself. Jimmy was incensed at what had taken place. Our insurance company eventually had to pay for the accident.

We heard about a program at Georgia Tech for handicapped students. Scotty went to take the test for admission and quit before it was over. Jimmy and I were very disappointed, because we really believed this might be the answer. How many more disappointments will be encountered before Scotty finds his niche?

Jimmy and Scotty had a verbal fight over Scotty's seeming lack of motivation. I checked out a video of Joni Eareckson Tada that told the story of how she and her family overcame the adversity of her diving accident which has left her a quadriplegic for life. Jimmy, Scotty and I watched it together and learned so much. After the video, Jimmy and Scotty hugged each other and asked for forgiveness while I cried.

Dr. O'Hara, another very helpful therapist, suggested Scotty get into some type of volunteer work involving sports. She called the Sports Information Department at Georgia Tech and they told Scotty to come and fill out an application.

Scotty was so excited to learn he had been accepted and would begin working there one day a week beginning in September. He couldn't wait to get started!

He basically delivered memos and messages between different coaches and athletic departments. He also gave free advice to Coach Bobby Ross, the Tech Head Football Coach, on how to improve his team. I'm sure Coach Ross really appreciated Scotty's uninvited counsel.

Scotty thoroughly enjoyed every minute of his work at Tech. He also liked the free football game tickets.

Scotty had always had a rough time admitting he was handicapped. A short time after beginning his work at Tech, he came to me and wanted me to apply for the handicapped sticker to place in the car. To me he was finally accepting the fact he had a handicap. Now, we could move on to more improvement in other areas which were designed to help the handicapped.

A beautiful verse of Scripture came to mind:

". . . being confident of this very thing, that he who has begun a good work in you will complete it until the day of Jesus Christ."

Philippians 1:6/NKJV)

During Christmas vacation of 1988, we decided it was time to go snow skiing. We flew to Colorado and checked into a condo Christmas day. Immediately after we arrived and were unloading our suitcases, the snow started falling in droves.

The next morning Jimmy rode the ski lift with Scotty for his first run down the slopes. Scotty did very well and by the end of the day was skiing with great skill. We were so proud and excited for Scotty. Scotty just loved it! What a fantastic week!

Scotty began a new job working at the Christian Life Center at our church, First Baptist of Cumming. Donald Wise, our youth director, suggested Scotty take the job of opening the Center for members to walk and jog each weekday morning. This really boosted Scotty's confidence in himself and in others.

Dr. Wolf, the physical therapist at Emory, suggested Scotty consider running in the Peachtree Road Race coming up on July 4th. At first, Scotty refused to even think about it. Then Dr. Wolf used some of his psychology and dared Scotty to try it. That did the trick, for Scotty was never one to back down from a challenge.

Dr. Wolf agreed to be his trainer and worked with him constantly. Scotty refused to wear a helmet, but later gave in to wearing knee and elbow pads.

Dr. Wolf also recommended I take Scotty to see the movie, *Rainman*. From what I had heard about the movie, I thought it might depress him, but I listened to the doctor and we went to see the movie.

As we watched the film, we laughed and cried together during several scenes. I didn't know what Scotty's response was going to be and was a bit anxious to hear his reaction.

He told me he really enjoyed the movie. He said he didn't realize he was doing so many things with his hands and his head that made him look like he was retarded. Jimmy and I had tried to relate this to him on many occasions, but Scotty just ignored us.

Now, he said he understood what we meant. He then asked me to help him correct the motions every time we detected one by simply saying, "Rainman." At that, he would know exactly what we were suggesting and try his best to rectify it.

We attended another Head Injury Foundation program and learned the University of Georgia had begun a program to help head injury victims obtain their education. I called for more information and found Scotty would have to be a transient student and his degree in business would have to be issued from Bryan College.

I then called the Bryan College Registrar's office and talked with Barbara Howard. She informed me Bryan would be more than happy to cooperate with the University of Georgia in finishing Scotty's degree.

Our whole family was just ecstatic about the prospects of this new found avenue for completing his business degree. Scotty was, of course, a little reluctant at taking such a major step, but later joined in our celebration.

I immediately began praying for a roommate that was just right for Scotty. We didn't know who it might be or where, but we knew when God opened a door, he always provides a way to walk through.

On March 1, 1989, we drove over to the University at Athens to discuss further the possibility of Scotty enrolling there. We spoke with personnel at the handicapped office and completed a form for housing request. Scotty was really overwhelmed by the magnitude of the campus. He didn't think he would ever find his way around. We just kept encouraging him to try it.

A few weeks later, Scotty was having a real down day. I had finished listening to a tape on "dealing with your insecurities." I told Scotty he should listen to it.

He did, and oh how he blessed me with his response to the cassette. He remarked after listening to the tape that he realized God had loaned him excellent health and his athletic abilities for a while. They belonged to Him, not Scotty, and God could take them back at His good pleasure and replace them with something else. Scotty then told me he should be thankful for the years God allowed him to use them. What incredible insight!

At the end of April, Scotty and I once again drove over to Athens to meet with special education personnel. We also met some of the professors Scotty would have. Scotty was not so intimidated at the vastness of the campus that time and seemed more to accept the fact he could do it.

We also visited Prince Avenue Baptist Church which we had heard was an excellent church. The people were so friendly. Scotty knew immediately where we would be worshiping in Athens.

Scotty had been working hard to read his Bible all the way through in a year. This particular morning he had read the verse in First Corinthians about disciplining your body.

> . . . But I discipline my body and bring it into subjection, lest, when I have preached to others, I myself should become disqualified.
> I Corinthians 9:27/NIV

He said it really spoke to him about working harder and harder to improve his body.

He and Dr. Wolf had been running more each time they got together. Scotty was really beginning to get excited about the Peachtree Road Race coming up in less than three months. Dr. Wolf said he would be ready. Scotty wasn't so sure.

He was having problems with blood blisters on his toes. They looked awful, but Scotty was determined to keep on. He was running more than five miles a day.

On Saturday, June 3rd, Scotty completed reading his entire Bible in a year. He was very proud and so were we. It really seemed to build his faith in God as well as in himself.

months. Dr. Wolf said he would be back.

Scotty would be sure.

He was having problems with the letters to his boss. They too showed what Scotty was so rubbed up. Keep on. He was reading more than five until Friday.

On Saturday June the people completed reading his sense Bible this year. He was very broad and every week in early seemed to build his up in God as well as in himself.

CHAPTER TEN

The University
of Georgia

ABOUT A WEEK before Scotty was to leave for Athens, he began to have an incredible fear of failure. He also wasn't too excited about living in the dorm with someone he had never met.

He drove around the campus, then parked his car near the Baptist Student Union. While walking in front of BSU, he met an interesting young man named Tim Hatch. After explaining his lack of enthusiasm at living in the dorm, Tim said he might have a place for him in a rented house.

We met Tim Hatch, a fine Christian young man who rented a house adjoining the campus and just behind the Baptist Student Union building. He invited Scotty to be his roommate and Scotty accepted. Having a

Christian roommate was a real answer to prayer.

The house had one bedroom, which Tim used. Scotty would live in the living room with a shower curtain separating him from another roommate who would live in the dining room. The house wasn't much, but would be adequate for Scotty's studies.

On Sunday, June 18th, Jimmy had to work, so Scotty and I packed the van very tightly and left for Athens. When we arrived at the house, I was concerned because there was no air conditioning. Scotty had been having some allergy problems and I didn't know if he could tolerate the heat. The house was also very dirty and needed a thorough cleaning. I spent the next day working on that. There were no locks on the doors, which didn't make me feel too good either.

I left Scotty about nine o'clock that evening. I cried most of the way home, but then I prayed and placed him in God's most capable hands once again.

That same evening after I had gone to bed, the phone rang at about eleven o'clock. It was Scotty and he spoke very softly as he tried to explain how someone was breaking into his house. He said he was awakened by a rock thrown through the living room window which just happened to be right above his bed. Scotty was terrified.

I told him to hang up the phone and I would call the Athens Police and then call him right back. I called the police and immediately returned the call to Scotty. I remained on the phone with Scotty until the police arrived some ten minutes later.

The police believed the whole incident was just a prank probably played on the wrong house, They didn't think there was any intention to harm Scotty. I agreed with them and they left about thirty minutes later. I stayed on the phone with Scotty until one o'clock in the morning when we both mutually consented he would be safe until I arrived there the next morning. What was God trying to teach us through this latest episode in Scotty's life? Probably nothing but to just trust Him.

I drove into the driveway of his house the following morning and Scotty had already showered. He seemed to be calm and shrugged off the previous night's incident.

We attended orientation and received his I.D. card and meal ticket. We bought his books, parking permit and everything else we could think of before five o'clock that evening. Now Scotty was ready to begin classes the next day.

His classes went very well. He was assigned someone to take notes for him as well as having a tutor for each class to help him keep pace with the rest of the students.

Scotty continued to work very hard in preparation for the Peachtree Road Race. He came home to run with Dr. Wolf twice each week and gained strength and endurance each practice. Scotty really didn't enjoy running that much, but he did like a challenge and still does.

He walked through our door at about five o'clock on the evening of July 3rd, the day before the big race. Dr. Wolf had already explained to us what Scotty should eat for dinner, but Scotty wanted to take a nap first.

Our daughter, Donna, and her husband, Dean, drove in from Gastonia, North Carolina, to watch Scotty run. We all sat down to dinner about six thirty and ate the pasta and other foods Dr. Wolf had recommended. We were so excited about the next morning and had a rough time getting to sleep that night. But we did.

Scotty got out of bed forty-five minutes before we were to leave and was primed and pumped to run the race. When we arrived at the starting line, Scotty and Dr. Wolf received their entrant numbers along with the other twenty-eight thousand contestants.

The wheelchair racers began first. What an inspiring sight to see handicapped men and women straining every muscle in their bodies to propel their wheelchairs.

From our vantage point at about the six mile marker, we saw many runners collapse from heat exhaustion. The sun was beating down relentlessly as volunteers passed cups of water to heavily perspiring runners. These men and women all looked to be in peak physical condition. How in the world would Scotty finish the race?

Just before Scotty reached the six mile marker, he told Dr. Wolf he just couldn't make it to the finish line. Dr. Wolf was beginning to run out of new words of inspiration when out of nowhere an older man jogged up next to Scotty. Instead of passing Scotty and finishing, he slowed down and gave him new words of encouragement and began to run with he and Dr. Wolf.

Scotty's legs were like jelly, but now he was revitalized. He would exert every ounce of energy left in his exhausted and fatigued body to cover the next half mile to the finish line.

Of course he was the last runner to pass us, but we cheered as if he were leading all twenty-eight thousand contestants. When he realized who was making all the whoopla over him, he motioned his hand for us to pipe down, because we were embarrassing him. We applauded and shouted even louder.

When Scotty crossed the finish line, he just sat down in the middle of the street. Medics darted toward him with a stretcher and asked if he was O.K. Scotty just shouted, "Get that thing out of here, I'm fine!"

Then the public address system blared out, "Ladies and gentlemen, that young man who just finished is Scott Hunt. He's been preparing for the Peachtree for months which his trainer, Dr. Steven Wolf. How about a round of applause for Scott Hunt."

Scotty was a little disappointed his time for the race wasn't fast enough to receive the 20th Anniversary T-shirt. Then an official approached us and said that they had to give Scotty a T-shirt anyway. Scotty was so proud of that shirt.

As Dr. Wolf helped him to his feet, they turned to see other runners cross the line. Scotty didn't finish last after all.

He walked gingerly over to a place on the grass where family and friends were gathered and sat down again. We all congregated around to congratulate him. He immediately took off his elbow pads, his knee pads and his sweat bands and threw them into the garbage can. Then he shouted, "That's over with. Never again."

A few days later in the Atlanta Journal sports sections, a headline read:

He Beat the Odds — Again!

AFTER RECOVERING FROM A COMA OF 62 DAYS, CRASH VICTIM RELEARNED HOW TO WALK, THEN RAN THE RACE OF HIS LIFE.

If was a beautiful article briefly retelling Scotty's story to that point in his life. What a tribute to hard work and strong determination. Once again, Thank you, Lord!

CHAPTER ELEVEN
More Tragedy!

THE NEXT WEEK Jimmy and I traveled with my sister and her husband up to the North Georgia mountains. When we returned home, we noticed an unfamiliar car parked in our driveway. We rushed into the house to find Scotty and Ron Little, the director of the University of Georgia Baptist Student Union sitting on the couch. Just when you thought Scotty had experienced enough tragedy for a lifetime, there appeared yet more!

Scotty had been asleep in his room at the house in Athens. He was harshly awakened by an enormously loud boom. He got out of bed, looked around and saw nothing. He then shouted for his other roommate, Kerry, whom we hadn't met yet, and received no response.

Scotty walked to the curtain separating their living quarters and peered around their edge to witness the most gruesome sight of his young lift. There lay Kerry on his bed, with blood gushing from his head and a revolver in his hand at his side. Scotty didn't touch anything, ran next door and had a neighbor call the police.

The police arrived and fingerprinted Scotty as if he were a suspect. His slurred speech led them to believe he may have been drunk, until Ron appeared and vouched for him. Ron had driven him to our house and here they were.

We thanked Ron profusely, and he was on his way back to Athens. Scotty retired to bed, but had a horrible time sleeping. He said he kept waking up with that horrendous sight of Kerry in his bed.

A short while later, Ron Little called and told us Scotty was welcome to use the guest room at the BSU until the end of the month in order to search for new living accommodations.

We returned to Athens on Thursday and moved Scotty's things out of the house and into the BSU. His professors told him he could drop out for the quarter or continue his studies — they would work with him anyway he wanted.

We discussed the situation and Scotty decided he wanted to continue his studies with no interruption. The next morning Scotty started back to class while Jimmy and I began looking for an apartment.

We found a suitable apartment for Scotty to live in beginning the first of August. Tim Hatch, Scotty's other Christian roommate, decided he didn't want to continue living in that house and asked to share a two bedroom apartment with Scotty. This worked out just great.

Tim was a fine Christian and spent most of his leisure time sharing his faith with young people at different camps and conferences. On one such retreat in Alabama, he told Scotty he had shared the story of his life from high school through the suicide of their roommate. Twelve young persons gave their lives to Christ that same night directly related to the testimony of Scotty's faith and determination in Christ.

Scotty took this first accounting test. He blew it royally and really got down on himself. The professor was very gracious and agreed to give Scotty the test orally. The results turned out to be an eighty-five. Scotty was so excited.

Professor Clark had never known Scotty, but yet was willing to work with him above and beyond his responsibility. Thank you Professor Clark.

Scotty had his twenty-fifth birthday and was honored with a surprise party given by about twenty of his friends. It had also been four years since the accident. Thank you, Lord, for bringing us this far.

Scotty came home for his summer break and was a great help around the house. He cut the grass, painted the decks, and anything else he could find to do.

Dr. Wolf and his family visited our house for lunch and some skiing on the lake. He and Scotty got alone while the rest of us went down to the lake. Dr. Wolf had been an incredible sounding board for Scotty that past year. Scotty left for school early in the evening and Dr. Wolf related to us some of what they had discussed. The most encouraging words he spoke were the fact Scotty still has so much more potential to keep improving himself. He also said Scotty was a most unusual young man and one for whom he had great respect.

Tim Hatch, Scotty's Christian roommate, decided to transfer to the University of South Alabama at Mobile to be Assistant Basketball Coach and pursue his Master's Degree. This left Scotty without a roommate and caused me great concern about his loneliness.

God provided a roommate, Greg Henzelman, who was a Campus Crusade for Christ staff member. Greg and Scotty became good friends. God always provides.

Scotty was a bit worried about his grades when he came home for Christmas break. Then he received them — two C's — and was tickled to death. No, they were not what he had been used to attaining before the accident, but he knew they were a pretty good assessment of what he was capable of doing now!

Scotty attended a conference with eleven hundred other college students. The speaker was Josh McDowell and he truly blessed Scotty with his words of wisdom and encouragement for students.

Tim Hatch came to visit us during Christmas and it was great to see him. He gave Scotty the challenge of considering going with Athletes In Action for the summer. Athletes In Action sends several athletic teams to foreign countries every summer and Scotty could be a member of one of their teams as a statistician. He sent out letters to friends and relatives to ask for their financial and prayer support for his venture with AIA. We were so thankful for the great response to this summer mission program for Scotty.

Chapter Twelve

Graduation from Bryan College

SCOTTY WOULD NOT FINISH his courses at Georgia until June 17th and Bryan's graduation was on Saturday, May 12th. The registrars department at Bryan told us they would love for Scotty to go through graduation exercises even though he would not officially graduate until they received his final grades from Georgia.

What a beautiful and exciting day May 12th was. We arrived at the Rudd Memorial Chapel on Bryan's campus at eight forty-five to claim our seats for the ten o'clock graduation service. We renewed acquaintances with Scotty's former professors, staff members and other friends who had been so very faithful during the past almost five years.

Then the moment we had all been hoping, praying and frankly, wondering if it would ever happen, did. Dr. Bill Brown, the Provost of the college and Scotty's former professor and friend, called out, "David Scott Hunt."

Scotty ambled up the steps and across the stage to a thundering round of applause. By the time he reached the podium at the center of the stage, the entire graduating class, faculty, student body and all in attendance were standing. It was a spontaneous ovation we will never forget.

As Scotty turned to face the audience, tears were streaming down his face, as well as most of the faculty and staff on the stage behind him. It is a long time honored tradition for every Bryan College graduate to quote his favorite verse of Scripture at graduation. Scotty held up his hands like a quarterback standing over his center to stop the ovation being given him. Then he tried to compose himself to quote his verses.

He finally began, "Some verses that have really become special to me are found in Second Corinthians 4:8-10. 'We are hard pressed on every side, yet not crushed.'" At this point his voice began to crack with emotion as the tears continued to stream from his eyes. He continued, "We are perplexed, but not in despair; persecuted, but not forsaken;

cast down, but not destroyed — always bearing about in the body the dying of the Lord Jesus, that the life also of Jesus might be made manifest in our body." (KJV)

"That says so much to me. For those of you that don't know me, these verses really say so much to me. I've been taken down a few notches the past few years and these verses mean so much. I also have here in my pocket a list of people I would like to thank." Scotty reached under his black robe and pulled a computer printout which was about two inches thick. The audience roared with laughter as he unfurled the mass of paper on the pulpit. "No, I'm just kidding, thanks a lot. See you later."

Scotty then proceeded to the other side of the stage to the loving and proud arms of Jimmy and myself. Jimmy handed Scotty the hood of his degree and the crowd, once again, applauded and gave Scotty another standing ovation as we walked him back to his seat. Thank you, Lord, for Your tender mercies.

Our son-in-law, Dean Vonfeldt, had accompanied us to Bryan for the first time at Scotty's graduation. He attended a large secular university and always wondered why Scotty insisted on returning to a small college like Bryan to finish his degree. After seeing first hand the love and beautiful interaction between the students, faculty, staff and parents, he understood why.

Scotty left in June for his mission trip to South America. He had a wonderful experience that helped him to grow in the Lord. His faith was stretched and he gained new confidence in himself.

Scotty was so impressed with Athletes In Action and Campus Crusade for Christ that he felt he wanted to go full-time with their ministry. He sent in his application and traveled to Colorado Springs, Colorado to visit some friends and other staff members he had met. He was so excited about the possibility of going to serve the Lord with Campus Crusade.

He attended another session that lasted for a month with Campus Crusade at their headquarters in Arrowhead Springs, California. This time in California would prove to Crusade whether or not they would accept him on staff.

The month flew by a lot faster than Scotty anticipated and he had a wonderful experience. Then on the day of his return home, officials at Campus Crusade informed Scotty they would not be able to use him on staff. This came as a real blow to Scotty and to Jimmy and me. Although we couldn't understand Crusades' decision, we had to believe God was in control.

We told Scotty that God had a better job for him somewhere else, but we had no idea where to turn next. We knew God had a particular vocation for Scotty. We just had to let Him lead us to it.

Scotty spent most of his day-light hours performing temporary odd jobs. At the same time he completed applications and attended numerous interviews.

Kent Robson, a man whom I had met at a Joni Eareckson Tada conference for the handicapped, had Scotty speak at his church. After hearing Scotty's testimony, he told Scotty he felt sure he had a place for him working with FCS (Family Consultation Service) Urban Ministries.

On Friday, April 5th, Scotty called me from the FCS offices and said he had accepted a job to start working in their Urban Ministries Division on the following Monday. Praise the Lord! Scotty would finally be going to work, and in full-time Christian ministry. Once again, he had to raise his own support. Within two months God laid his support on the hearts of many friends and relatives and his complete financial resources for the next year were met in faithful pledges.

Scotty now has an apartment in Stone Mountain and rides the MARTA (Metropolitan Atlanta Rapid Transit Authority) Train to his office in downtown Atlanta. He drives anywhere he wants and eats a lot of microwave dinners. He loves sharing his testimony with youth groups and churches all over the Atlanta area.

His speech and walking continue to improve. When we were discussing a title of this book, we asked Scotty how he liked, "Why Scotty?"

He responded, "Yes, but does it answer the question?"

We still haven't found all the answers to why God allowed Scotty and ourselves to live through the past seven years. One evening we were visiting with Colonel Bill Kehler whose son was a cadet at the Air Force Academy in Colorado Springs. His boy was a fine Christian with a terrific future ahead of him. Tim had been killed in a bombing mission. After talking with Bill for a while, Scotty asked him, "Why Tim?"

Colonel Kehler replied, "Why not Tim?"

Chuck Colson, one of Nixon's hatchet men and now Chairman of the Board of Prison Fellowship, once said something that makes a lot of sense. He said he believed every time a non-Christian gets cancer, God allows a Christian to get cancer just to show the world how a Christian can handle it through his faith in Christ.

That simple, yet profound statement really ministered to Scotty, Jimmy and me. We may not ever understand what or why God allows his children to rejoice and sometimes to suffer. But the Jimmy Hunt family knows for a fact, "His grace is sufficient, for His strength is made perfect in weakness" (2 Corinthians 12:9).

In closing, let me leave you with one more portion of Scripture that is our constant hope and prayer:

> "So, whatever it takes, I will be one who lives in the fresh newness of life of those who are alive from the dead. I don't mean to say I am perfect. I haven't learned all I should even yet, but I keep working toward that day when I will finally be all that Christ saved me for and wants me to be. No, dear brothers, I am still not all I should be, but I am bringing all my energies to bear on this one thing: Forgetting the past and looking forward to what lies ahead . . . ."
>
> Philippians 3:11-13/LB

Jesus is Lord!

EPILOGUE

HOW TO KNOW CHRIST

If you are not sure of your relationship with God and want to begin a daily walk with Jesus Christ, just simply follow these steps:

1. **Believe** —
   A. God loves you and wants you to have the best life possible.

   B. Sin (disobeying God's laws) keeps you from knowing God's best for your life.

   C. God's Son, Jesus Christ, died on the cross for your sins, making it possible for you to know Him personally.

   D. You must invite Jesus Christ to come into your life and take control of it.

2. Pray —

Bow your head and talk to God, saying this simple prayer:

God, I believe that You sent Your Son, Jesus Christ, to make full payment for my sins by His death on the cross. I ask You to forgive me of all my sins and come and live within my heart.

If you prayed this prayer, the Bible, God's Holy Word, promises that Jesus Christ is now in your heart. Tell your relatives, friends and everyone you know, what you have done. Write to me at the address below and we will send you more information on how to continue your daily walk with Jesus Christ.

Wynell Hunt
3570 Strawberry Lane
Cumming, Georgia 30131

or write my co-author

Terry Hill
1202 N. W. Rutland Road
Mt. Juliet, Tennessee 37122

Full Court Press is a Christian
publisher committed to the ethical
proclamation of the "GoodNews"
of Jesus Christ.

For information or to order write:
  Full Court Press
  P.O. Box 141513
  Grand Rapids, MI 49514